La

Life Story of a
Butterfly

Charlotte Guillain

raintree

a Capstone company

Raintree is an imprint of Capstone Global Library Limited, a company incorporated in England and Wales having its registered office at 7 Pilgrim Street, London, EC4V 6LB – Registered company number: 6695582

www.raintreepublishers.co.uk
myorders@raintreepublishers.co.uk

Edited by Catherine Veitch and Gina Kammer
Designed by Richard Parker and Peggie Carley
Picture research by Mica Brancic
Production by Victoria Fitzgerald
Originated by Capstone Global Library Ltd
Printed and bound in China by Leo Paper Group

ISBN 978 1 406 28232 0 (hardback)
18 17 16 15 14
10 9 8 7 6 5 4 3 2 1

ISBN 978 1 406 28237 5 (paperback)
19 18 17 16 15
10 9 8 7 6 5 4 3 2

British Library Cataloguing in Publication Data
A full catalogue record for this book is available from the British Library.

Acknowledgements
We would like to thank the following for permission to reproduce photographs:

Alamy: Don Johnston, 9, Eric Carr, 20, Marvin Dembinsky Photo Associates, 12, 28 (right), Survivalphotos, 8, 24, 28 (left); FLPA: Minden Pictures/Ingo Arndt, 19, 22; Getty Images: Kerri Wile, 27, Oxford Scientific/Ed Reschke, cover; Science Source: E. R. Degginger, 7, Eileen Tanson, 11, Phil Degginger, 15, 29 (left), Scott Camazine, 14, Stuart Wilson, 16; Shutterstock: AlexussK (stone design element), cover and throughout, Cathy Keifer, 10, 13, Cynthia Kidwell, 21, 29 (right), Hurst Photo, 23, jannoon028 (grass border), throughout, kingfisher, 17, Leighton Photography & Imaging, 5, Melola, 18, Sari ONeal, 4, wizdata, 6, Yuliya Proskurina (green leaves border), cover and throughout; SuperStock: Minden Pictures, 25, 26

We would like to thank Michael Bright for his assistance in the preparation of this book.

Every effort has been made to contact copyright holders of material reproduced in this book. Any omissions will be rectified in subsequent printings if notice is given to the publisher.

Contents

Some words are shown in bold, **like this**. You can find out what they mean by looking in the glossary.

What is a butterfly?

A butterfly is a type of animal called an **insect.** Insects are animals with three pairs of legs and a body with three main parts. Many insects have wings.

There are many types of butterflies. They live in many places around the world and can be different sizes and colours.

A butterfly's life story

Like all other animals, a butterfly goes through different stages as it grows into an adult. These stages make up an animal's life story.

young

adult

Follow the life story of butterflies, and watch them change in unusual ways as they develop and grow.

It starts with an egg

A butterfly starts its life as an egg. The egg is oval shaped, tiny, and white.

A butterfly's mother usually lays one egg under a leaf. A sticky substance holds the egg onto the plant.

The egg hatches

After three to five days the **larva** starts to hatch from the egg.

A butterfly larva is usually called a caterpillar.
This tiny caterpillar is pale, with a dark head
to start with. As it grows it changes colour.

A growing caterpillar

The caterpillar starts to eat. First it eats its own egg, and then it starts to feed on the plants around it. It gets bigger and bigger.

The caterpillar grows so much that its skin splits several times. When its skin splits, the caterpillar crawls out with a soft new skin.

Changing into a pupa

When a caterpillar is very fat, it cannot grow any bigger. It makes a sticky liquid and attaches itself to a twig or leaf.

chrysalis

The caterpillar's skin splits one more time.
A **pupa** is now underneath. The pupa has
a hard shell. A pupa is sometimes called a
chrysalis.

The stage when a caterpillar changes into an adult is called a pupa. This change of body shape is called **metamorphosis**.

cloudless sulphur butterfly pupa

monarch
butterfly
pupa

It takes a monarch butterfly about 10 days to turn into an adult. Other butterflies can take months to change into adults.

Changing into an adult

When a pupa has changed into an adult butterfly, the shell around it splits open. It slowly comes out of the shell.

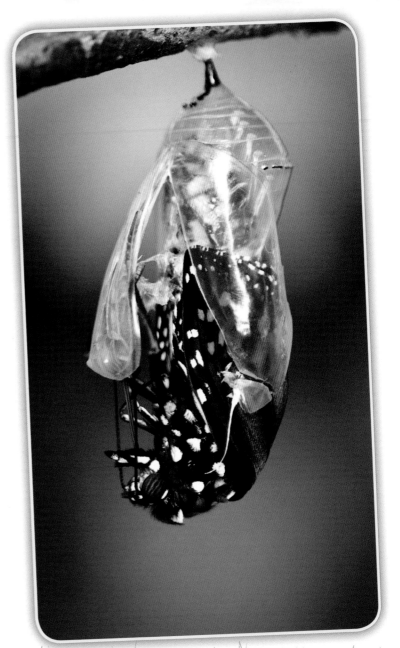

The adult butterfly's wings are soft and damp at first. It has to wait a few hours for its wings to dry and its body to get harder.

Like all insects, an adult butterfly has three body parts. These are the head, the **thorax**, and the **abdomen**.

head

thorax

abdomen

antennae

proboscis

On a butterfly's head there are two eyes and two **antennae**, which it uses to smell food. In its mouth is a long tube called a **proboscis**, which it uses to suck up food.

Mating

The butterfly looks for a mate, so they can continue the life story. Together they can **reproduce** and create new butterflies.

A female butterfly uses its **antennae** to smell a chemical that a male butterfly makes when it is ready to mate.

After the male and female butterflies have mated, the female is ready to lay eggs. It will usually do this in spring, when the weather is warm.

When a female butterfly has laid eggs on a plant, it leaves them. Sometimes a **predator**, such as an ant, will eat the eggs before they hatch.

A butterfly's life

A butterfly cannot live in places that have very cold weather. It flies south to a warmer place to spend the winter.

Most adult butterflies do not live longer than a month. Many butterflies are eaten by predators, such as birds, other insects, and frogs.

Butterfly life story diagram

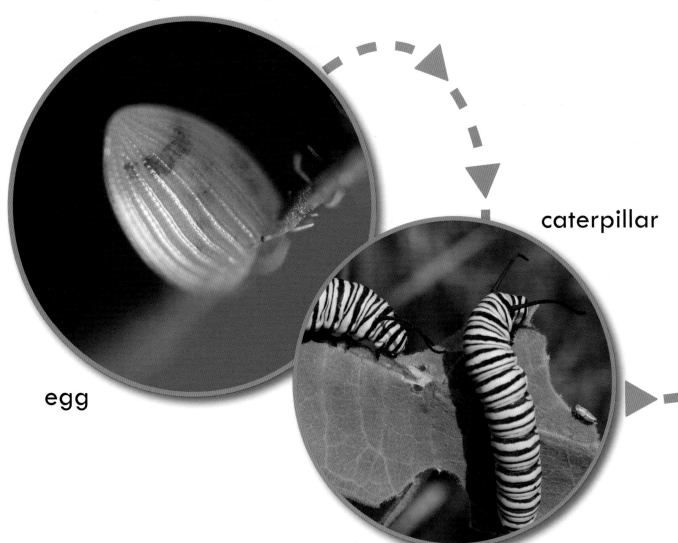

egg

caterpillar

butterfly

chrysalis

Glossary

abdomen lower part of an insect's body, which is joined to the thorax

antennae long, thin feelers on an insect's head that it uses to feel and smell

chrysalis stage of an insect's life when it changes from a larva to an adult; also known as a pupa

insect type of animal with no backbone that has three main body parts and three pairs of legs

larva stage in an animal's life before it becomes an adult

metamorphosis stages where an animal changes body shape and appearance

predator animal that hunts and eats other animals

proboscis long mouthpart, like a tube, that sucks up food

pupa stage of an insect's life when it changes from a larva to an adult

reproduce to lay eggs or give birth to young

thorax part of an insect's body between the head and abdomen

Find out more

Books

A Monarch Butterfly's Journey, Suzanne Slade
(Picture Window Books, 2012)

Butterflies and Moths, Clare Hibbert
(Arcturus Publishing, 2011)

Sensational Butterflies Sticker Book
(Natural History Museum, 2013)

Websites

http://www.bbc.co.uk/nature/life/Lepidoptera
Visit the BBC Nature website to find out more
about butterflies and watch video clips.

**http://kids.nationalgeographic.com/kids/
animals/creaturefeature/monarch-butterflies/**
Visit the National Geographic website to find out
about Monarch butterflies.

Index